Poetry for Students, Volume 1

Staff

Marie Rose Napierkowski and Mary K. Ruby, *Editors*

David J. Kelly, Paul Mooney, Alan R. Velie, *Contributing Writers*

Gerald Barterian, Suzanne Dewsbury, David Galens, Jennifer Gariepy, Marie Lazzari, Tom Ligotti, Anna J. Sheets, Lynn M. Spampinato, Diane Telgen, Lawrence J. Trudeau, Kathleen Wilson, *Contributing Editors*

Michael L. LaBlanc, *Managing Editor*

Jeffery Chapman, *Programmer/Analyst*

Victoria B. Cariappa, *Research Team Manager*
Michele P. LaMeau, Andy Guy Malonis, Barb McNeil, Gary Oudersluys, Maureen Richards, *Research Specialists*
Julia C. Daniel, Tamara C. Nott, Tracie A.

Richardson, Cheryl L. Warnock, *Research Associates*

Susan M. Trosky, *Permissions Manager*
Kimberly F. Smilay, *Permissions Specialist*
Sarah Chesney, *Permissions Associate*
Steve Cusack, Kelly A. Quin, *Permissions Assistants*

Mary Beth Trimper, *Production Director*
Evi Seoud, *Assistant Production Manager*
Shanna Heilveil, *Production Assistant*

Randy Bassett, *Image Database Supervisor*
Mikal Ansari, Robert Duncan, *Imaging Specialists*
Pamela A. Reed, *Photography Coordinator*

Cynthia Baldwin, *Product Design Manager*
Cover design: Michelle DiMercurio, *Art Director*
Page design: Pamela A. E. Galbreath, *Senior Art Director*

Gale Research
835 Penobscot Building
645 Griswold St.
Detroit, MI 48226-4094

This book is printed on acid-free paper that meets the minimum requirements of American National Standard for Information Sciences—Permanence Paper for Printed Library Materials, ANSI Z39.48-1984.

ISBN 0-7876-1688-5
ISSN 1094-7019

Printed in the United States of America
10 9 8 7

The Love Song of J. Alfred Prufrock

T. S. Eliot

1915

Introduction

Segments of "The Love Song of J. Alfred Prufrock," often called "the first Modernist poem," appeared in the *Harvard Advocate* in 1906 while Eliot was an undergraduate. He later read the poem to Ezra Pound in England and Pound arranged to have it published in the prestigious American journal *Poetry* in June 1915. It was included in *Prufrock and Other Observations,* Eliot's first book of poetry, in 1917.

Eliot's interest in music is made evident in the

title, but the term "love song" is used loosely here. The poem centers on the feelings and thoughts of the persona, J. Alfred Prufrock, as he walks to meet a woman for tea and considers a question he feels compelled to ask her (something along the lines of "Will you marry me?"). In fact, in this poem he never arrives at tea, let alone sings to the woman. The poem is composed of Prufrock's own neurotic —if lyrical—associations. Indeed, over the course of the poem, he sets up analogies between himself and various familiar cultural figures, among them Hamlet. This establishes a connection with Hamlet's famous soliloquy ('To be or not to be?—That is the question"). Prufrock's doubt that he deserves the answer he desires from this woman transforms the poem into a kind of interior monologue or soliloquy in which "To be or not to be?" is for Prufrock "To be what?" and "What or who am I to ask this woman to marry me?"

Seen as simply the romantic agonizing of a young man (Eliot was eighteen when he began the poem) over a woman he loves, "The Love Song of J. Alfred Prufrock" would have a distinctly limited appeal. However, the poem moves from this specific situation to explore the peculiarly Modernist alienation of the individual in society to a point where internal emotional alienation occurs and a soliloquy in which a man speaks *as if alone* can begin, "Let us go then, you and I...."

Author Biography

Eliot was born in 1888 in St. Louis, Missouri, a member of a distinguished family that included Puritan ancestors who had been original settlers of Massachusetts. In 1906 Eliot entered Harvard University. He served on the staff of the *Harvard Advocate,* the university's literary journal, in which he first published parts of "The Love Song of J. Alfred Prufrock." He completed his undergraduate studies in 1909 and his master's degree in English literature the following year. Over the next six years Eliot pursued graduate studies in philosophy at the Sorbonne, Harvard, Marburg, and Oxford, completing his dissertation in 1916. During this time Eliot met Ezra Pound, who became his lifelong friend and an important literary influence. In 1915, while studying in England, Eliot met and later married an Englishwoman named Vivien Haigh-Wood. Their marriage has generally been characterized as unhappy, troubled by Vivien's neurotic illnesses and Eliot's sexual apprehensions. The couple settled in London, and Eliot began teaching at a boy's school while writing reviews for various periodicals and composing poetry. In 1917 Eliot left teaching and began working at Lloyd's Bank; however, he continued to follow his literary pursuits, publishing *Prufrock and Other Observations* in 1917 and becoming an assistant editor for the journal the *Egoist.* The combined strain of his failing marriage and the pressures from his banking and writing careers resulted in Eliot's emotional breakdown in 1921. He sought treatment at a sanitorium in Switzerland, where he completed *The Waste Land* in 1922. Returning to London, Eliot became the founding editor of a new literary journal, the *Criterion,* in which he published *The Waste Land.* The *Criterion* is now recognized as one of the most distinguished periodicals in the twentieth century.

After having lived in England for over a decade, in 1927 Eliot became a British subject and a member of the Anglican Church. Five years later, he received a one-year appointment to the Charles Eliot Norton professorship at Harvard and subsequently lectured at major universities throughout the United States. Also during the 1930s Eliot began devoting much of his time to writing verse dramas. During World War II Eliot wrote his last major poetic works, *East Coker*(1940), *Burnt Norton*(1941), *The Dry Salvages*(1941), and *Little Gidding*(1942, together published as *Four Quartets)*. Eliot experienced marked changes in his personal life beginning in 1947, when Vivien died after having spent several years in an institution. He subsequently met Valerie Fletcher, who became his secretary and later his wife, and with whom he enjoyed a stable and happy relationship for the rest of his life. In 1948 Eliot received both the Nobel Prize for Literature and the Order of Merit by George VI, both honors—along with his newfound popularity as a dramatist—augmenting his stature as a celebrated literary figure which he maintained until his death in 1965. Eliot is buried in Poet's

Corner of Westminster Abbey.

Poem Text

S'io credesse che mia risposta fosse
A persona che mai tornasse al mondo,
Questa fiamma staria senza piu scosse.

Ma perciocche giammai di questo fondo
Non torno vivo alcun, s'i'odo il vero,
Senza tema d'infamia ti rispondo.

Let us go then, you and I,
When the evening is spread out against the sky
Like a patient etherised upon a table;
Let us go, through certain half-deserted streets,
The muttering retreats
Of restless nights in one-night cheap hotels
And sawdust restaurants with oyster-shells:
Streets that follow like a tedious argument
Of insidious intent
To lead you to an overwhelming question ...
Oh, do not ask, "What is it?"
Let us go and make our visit.

In the room the women come and go
Talking of Michelangelo.

The yellow fog that rubs its back upon the
window-panes.

The yellow smoke that rubs its muzzle on the
window-panes

Licked its tongue into the corners of the evening,
Lingered upon the pools that stand in drains,
Let fall upon its back the soot that falls from
chimneys,
Slipped by the terrace, made a sudden leap,
And seeing that it was a soft October night,
Curled once about the house, and fell asleep.

And indeed there will be time
For the yellow smoke that slides along the street,
Rubbing its back upon the window-panes;
There will be time, there will be time
To prepare a face to meet the faces that you meet;

There will be time to murder and create,
And time for all the works and days of hands
That lift and drop a question on your plate;
Time for you and time for me,
And time yet for a hundred indecisions,
And for a hundred visions and revisions,
Before the taking of a toast and tea.

In the room the women come and go
Talking of Michelangelo.

And indeed there will be time
To wonder, "Do I dare?" and, "Do I dare?"
Time to turn back and descend the stair,
With a bald spot in the middle of my hair—
[They will say: "How his hair is growing thin!"]
My morning coat, my collar mounting firmly to the
chin,
My necktie rich and modest, but asserted by a
simple pin—
[They will say: "But how his arms and legs are

thin!"]
Do I dare
Disturb the universe?
In a minute there is time
For decisions and revisions which a minute will
reverse.

For I have known them all already, known
them all:—
Have known the evenings, mornings, afternoons,
I have measured out my life with coffee spoons;
I know the voices dying with a dying fall
Beneath the music from a farther room.
So how should I presume?

And I have known the eyes already, known
them all—
The eyes that fix you in a formulated phrase,
And when I am formulated, sprawling on a pin,
When I am pinned and wriggling on the wall,
Then how should I begin
To spit out all the butt-ends of my days and ways?

And how should I presume?

And I have known the arms already, known them
all-
Arms that are braceleted and white and bare
[But in the lamplight, downed with light brown
hair!]
Is it perfume from a dress
That makes me so digress?
Arms that lie along a table, or wrap about a shawl.
And should I then presume?
And how should I begin?

.....

Shall I say, I have gone at dusk through narrow
streets
And watched the smoke that rises from the pipes
Of lonely men in shirt-sleeves, leaning out of
windows...?

I should have been a pair of ragged claws
Scuttling across the floors of silent seas.

.....

And the afternoon, the evening, sleeps so
peacefully!
Smoothed by long fingers,
Asleep ... tired ... or it malingers,
Stretched on the floor, here beside you and me.
Should I, after tea and cakes and ices.
Have the strength to force the moment to its crisis?
But though I have wept and fasted, wept and
prayed,
Though I have seen my head [grown slightly bald]
brought in upon a platter,
I am no prophet—and here's no great matter;
I have seen the moment of my greatness flicker,
And I have seen the eternal Footman hold my coat,
and snicker,
And in short, I was afraid.
And would it have been worth it, after all,
After the cups, the marmalade, the tea,

Among the porcelain, among some

talk of you and
me.
Would it have been worth while,
To have bitten off the matter with a
smile,
To have squeezed the universe into a
ball
To roll it toward some overwhelming
question,
To say: "I am Lazarus, come from
the dead,
Come back to tell you all, I shall tell
you all"—
If one, settling a pillow by her head,
Should say: "That is not what I
meant at all.
That is not it, at all."

And would it have been worth it,
after all,
Would it have been worth while,
After the sunsets and the dooryards
and the
sprinkled streets,
After the novels, after the teacups,
after the skirts
that trail along the
floor—
And this, and so much more?—
It is impossible to say just what I
mean!
But as if a magic lantern threw the
nerves in

patterns on a screen:
Would it have been worth while
If one, settling a pillow or throwing off a shawl,
And turning toward the window, should say:
"That is not it at all,
That is not what I meant, at all."

.....

No! I am not Prince Hamlet, nor was meant to be;
Am an attendant lord, one that will do
To swell a progress, start a scene or two,
Advise the prince; no doubt, an easy tool,
Deferential, glad to be of use,
Politic, cautious, and meticulous;
Full of high sentence, but a bit obtuse;
At times, indeed, almost ridiculous—
Almost, at times, the Fool.

I grow old ... I grow old ...
I shall wear the bottoms of my trousers rolled.

Shall I part my hair behind? Do I dare to eat a
peach?

I shall wear white flannel trousers, and walk upon
the beach.
I have heard the mermaids singing, each to each.
I do not think that they will sing to me.

I have seen them riding seaward on the waves
Combing the white hair of the waves blown back
When the wind blows the water white and black.

We have lingered in the chambers of the sea
By sea-girls wreathed with seaweed red and brown
Till human voices wake us, and we drown.

Poem Summary

Lines 1-6

This epigraph is taken from Dante's Divine Comedy. It reads: "If I thought my answer were to one who could ever return to the world, this flame would move no more; but since no one has ever returned alive from this depth, if what I hear be true, without fear of infamy I answer you." The words are spoken by a lost soul, damned to Hell for the attempt to buy absolution in advance of committing a crime. This correlates with Prufrock's need to know the answer to the question he wants to ask as a condition of asking it. Or perhaps in order for Prufrock to be able to ask the question he would have to not care what the answer would be; in that case, the answer wouldn't matter.

Media Adaptations

- "The Caedmon Treasury of Modern Poets Reading Their Own Poetry." Audio cassette. Audiobooks, order #4322.
- "More T.S. Eliot Reads." Audio cassette. Audiobooks, order #4388.
- "Old Possum's Book of Practical Cats, by T.S. Eliot." Audio cassette. Audiobooks, Order #4393.

Lines 7-9

Prufrock, the persona of the poem, issues his invitation to an unspecified "you" to go with him to an as yet unspecified place. To establish when they will be going, he introduces the disconcerting simile "like a patient etherised upon a table." This peculiar use of simile reflects immediately back on the persona, for the sky itself would probably never be *like* this; however, Prufrock, looking up at the sky, might indeed perceive it pressing back down upon him in such a way that he would feel like he was "spread out" "upon a table." The word "etherised" indicates a sense of helplessness.

Lines 10-13

The route he and the "you" will be taking is

through a tawdry part of the city where “cheap hotels” predominate, along with lower-class dining establishments. “Muttering retreats” suggests places where people who go to be alone speak in low voices so their private conversations will not be heard. The phrase “one-night” refers to hotels where lovers meet in secret, and the reference to “oyster-shells” carries with it the connotation of sexuality, as these are a food said to improve sexual stamina.

Lines 14-18

“Streets” are further described by a simile that indicates that even once you pass through them, the things you have seen there continue to affect you, specifically the idea of people engaged in the romantic or sexual encounters in the hotels and restaurants. This then affects Prufrock’s thoughts about where he is going, causing him to consider what he characterizes as an “overwhelming” question. The use of the ellipsis indicates that the “you” who accompanies Prufrock has asked what that question would be.

The rhymed couplets of “I-sky,” “streets-retreats,” “hotels-oyster-shells,” “argument-intent,” and ’“What is it?’-visit,” along with repetition of the word “streets,” create an emotional music in keeping with the idea of a song, and thus serve to carry the reader into Prufrock’s emotional state.

Lines 19-20

The reference to the visit presented in the preceding stanza causes Prufrock to look forward in his mind's eye to the room he is walking toward, where he imagines women preparing the tea and talking of some intellectual or artistic subject quite at odds with the thoughts he has been having.

Lines 21-28

The near repetition in lines 21 and 22 signals that Prufrock's attention has returned from the imagined room to his actual surroundings. It is evening, foggy, and his attention focuses on the fog mixed with chimney smoke, and then takes off in a metaphorical process that equates the movement of the fog with the movement of some seemingly cat-like creature around the structure of the city at evening. Prufrock's lyrical musing here reflects the dream-like emotional state evoked by the fog.

The lines in this stanza are very close in length, so that along with the rhyme pattern of *a a b a c d e d a,* and the alliteration of "[l]icked," "[l]ingered," and "leap," a kind of trancelike state is established.

Lines 29-40

Prufrock's reverie on the smoke or fog reminds him that dreamed or imagined activity has no correlation to actions or events in real time, so he determines that just as there is time for the fog and smoke, there is time to get himself adjusted to what he is about to do. However, at the fourth repetition of "There will be time" he is once more focusing on where he is going and what he is about to do there, and he is overwhelmed once again. Eliot exaggerates Prufrock's emotional state by paralleling it to those associated with acts of murder and creation. At this point the phrase "there will be time" transmutes into repetitions of the word "time" like a clock ticking the seconds of the present into Prufrock's past.

The reference to "works and days" is to an eighth century B.C. poem by Hesiod about a Greek farmer who urges his brother to work as hard as he himself does. Prufrock imagines other hands working harder than his, that will ultimately somehow necessitate his asking the "overwhelming question." However, he maintains he has time yet for a hundred dream-visions of cat-like fogs, for a hundred corrections to his thought process, before he arrives for tea.

Lines 41-42

The reference above to having tea presents him with the repeated image in the rhymed couplet.

Lines 43-50

Here Prufrock's thought process becomes infused with a sense of the ridiculous, as he pictures himself losing his resolve, turning and walking back down the stairs before even knocking on the door. The irony is that, seeing himself as silly, he begins to be aware of how others might see him, even to the point of including in the stream of his own thought (bracketed in the poem) disparaging comments that he imagines these others might make about him, comments that are in direct contradiction of how he sees himself.

Lines 51-54

Prufrock's third repetition of "Do I dare?" is exaggerated to reflect the depth of his own dread. He repeats that while there *is* time for all these thoughts, the situation is still hopeless: as long as it takes to make a decision is as long as it takes to reverse that decision.

Lines 55-60

Prufrock tries to explain *why* he is indecisive about his feelings toward the woman he is meeting for tea. It is because he knows the kind of social life he is moving toward. He knows how people who live together and have social obligations toward one another act—or are supposed to act. The visual image of the coffee spoons indicates that he himself has had innumerable cups of coffee in unbearable social situations. The aural image of the "voices dying" refers to difficult and embarrassing social conversations that falter while those involved pretend to be listening to music. And so, Prufrock asks himself, how can such a socially inept individual as he is ever hope to assume a part in real human life with this woman?

Lines 61-67

Prufrock indicates that he is familiar with people who appraise him according to some set of standards that have nothing to do with who he considers himself to be. Eliot uses metaphor here to illustrate that such appraisals make Prufrock incapable of human response because he feels as if he is as insignificant and helpless as a bug stuck by a pin for collection and examination. The image of the "butt-ends" are what he thinks his "days and ways" must be reduced to in order to explain what he does, as the "butt-ends" of cigarettes are what remains after the pleasure of smoking.

Lines 68-75

The tone softens here as Prufrock recalls a third thing that he has "known" as a result of social situations, symbolized by the image of feminine arms. These arms have a hint of the sensual in the bracketed information he provides that is suggestive of the earlier animal image of the fog as well as of the sexual associations of the hotels and restaurants. Prufrock realizes that this image of what he has "known" is at variance with those of the two preceding stanzas, and wonders what has shifted his thoughts. That it was the feminine appeal of a perfume he caught scent of continues the visual image of these arms, however, transforming the question asked at the end of each of those preceding stanzas. Now he asks, "Should I presume?" This implies that his desire for the female embrace is overriding his doubts. Indeed, the final line assumes he *will* "presume" by allowing him to consider "how" to begin.

Line 76

This ellipsis acts to divide the first two sections of the poem; it also indicates that there were thoughts resulting from the final question of the preceding stanza that neither Prufrock nor Eliot wants to consider further.

Lines 77-79

Eliot brings Prufrock and the reader back to the idea of how Prufrock might begin to talk to the woman he is going to meet. The image of "lonely men" symbolizes the loneliness of Prufrock. The use of an ellipsis within the sentence structure at the close of the stanza indicates further consideration, perhaps, of this loneliness, which is enhanced by the fact that these are the only two consecutive unrhymed lines in the poem.

Lines 80-81

Prufrock acknowledges what he feels to be the utter hopelessness of his situation. The image of the "ragged claws" in the "silent seas" suggests that, as a creature of a "higher order" Prufrock's brain is doing him no good at all. In fact, it is clear that Prufrock feels that his ability to speak—which supposedly establishes his superiority over all other animals—is so inferior that he should be relegated to a world of silence.

Line 82

The ellipsis here might mark further hopeless thoughts which have not been included, but more likely indicates the enormity of the realization Prufrock has just come to: his human life will be wasted as a result of his inability to participate fully in human relationships.

Lines 83-94

There is a definite shift in tone here, in keeping with the image of evening made peaceful by "long fingers" caressing it into sleep. The internal ellipses indicate reconsiderations, so that perhaps the evening and (by metaphorical process) Prufrock's emotions are not so much "peacefully" at rest, perhaps they are "tired," or worse, shirking their duty. In any case, it is the evening now which is cat-like "beside you and me." And here it seems as if "you" might be hopefully referring to the woman with whom Prufrock has presumably had tea. But this peacefulness is disrupted as Prufrock wonders if he "has the strength" to ask this woman the "overwhelming question."

Despite the fact that Prufrock has agonized over the situation, he does not know whether he will be able to ask his question or not. His association of this behavior with the weeping and fasting that

Biblical prophets were said to engage in establishes the basis for an analogy with the prophet John the Baptist. The irony is that it shouldn't take a prophet to tell you whether or not you yourself are going to do something. Eliot nicely accents this ironical stance by using the particular prophet John the Baptist, a proponent of chastity who was beheaded at the request of Herod's wife. Prufrock's sense of the ridiculousness of the situation once again asserts itself in the satiric inserted comment in the presentation of the image of his own head on the platter in place of John the Baptist's. Ultimately, though, it is clear to him that he is exaggerating, to no good effect, for the really important thing to consider is that he is no longer sure of himself as a human being. Accordingly, he is truly frightened at the image of the derision of the "eternal Footman"—which is, perhaps, death as a doorman holding Prufrock's coat and ushering him out of a life that he never had the courage to truly live.

Lines 95-106

Another question sets the tone for this stanza, as Prufrock considers whether he could ask his "overwhelming question" within the context of the social trivialities of having tea. The use here of the Egyptian religious symbol of the scarab beetle, which rolls its excrement into a ball, is an intricate image compounded of the vulgar and the divine. It precisely expresses Prufrock's view of his situation.

He also imagines himself, incongruously, as a

kind of Lazarus (whom Jesus raised from the dead) at this tea, who comes back from the dead place inside himself to tell this woman everything he learned there. But his imaginings carry him off to the point where he sees her casually asserting that his "overwhelming question" has nothing to do with anything that she said.

Lines 107-119

Prufrock's thinking begins to fragment as a result of his frustration and dread. The stanza begins with an echo of the first line of the preceding stanza, then repeats a variation that leads into a series of recollections in two lines beginning with "After" as Prufrock recites a series of events. In line 113 he acknowledges that he cannot say what he means.

It becomes clear with line 114 that Prufrock believes that he must adequately and specifically communicate the scope, the depth, the magnitude of what he thinks and feels about this woman so that the "meaning" he communicates will correspond with the "meaning" of something she has previously said or done. But he is so convinced that this will not happen that he can almost see her turning away from him. Eliot presents this with an image of his nerves projecting the picture of her failure to understand onto the screen of his imagination.

Line 120

Here the ellipsis again emphasizes the full

weight of what happens in this section, the sense of futility Prufrock experiences in the face of the impossibility of saying "just what I mean!" It further marks the transition into the state of mind that occurs after the full realization of this impossibility.

Lines 121-129

Prufrock emphatically answers the question he has asked in the preceding two stanzas. His reference to Hamlet, and the phrase in the same line, "nor was meant to be," calls up an association with Hamlet's soliloquy, "To be or not to be?—That is the question." Clearly there is a play on words here. On one level, the asking of the question and the establishing of the relationship with the woman is "not to be." On another level, Prufrock is suggesting that he is not "meant *to be,*" implying that he is meant, perhaps, merely to exist and never to really participate in life. On an existential level, the line could indicate that Prufrock is "meant" "*not to be,*" that he might as well be dead for not being able to live as people live.

Prufrock describes himself in a self-satiric way in lines 123-129, noting that his unimportant presence will help to fill out a crowd scene, and finally referring to himself as "obtuse," which means "ignorant" as well as "insensitive." Clearly, Prufrock is not "insensitive"; rather, he is far too sensitive. But he is ignorant of how social relationships provide structure for emotional life.

Prufrock determines that he will never be the main character in his own play, although he might have a function as "the Fool," or court jester, who can provide light entertainment. The word "Fool" also alludes to how foolish he is in his inaction.

Lines 130-131

The ellipses indicate the passage of time, as Prufrock feels himself growing older. Line 131 has been variously interpreted as having to do with some kind of fashion of the times, as well as pertaining to how people roll up their pant legs to keep from getting them wet as they walk on the shore. It could also be read as reference to getting shorter as one gets older, so that the trousers would need to be rolled up.

Lines 132-134

The questions Prufrock asks here are satiric versions of the serious question he tried to ask of the woman, and of the useless questions he has asked of himself. The satire is intensified with his image of himself as an old man who parts his hair "behind" in order to comb it forward over a receding hairline. The use of the rhymed couplet here is particularly interesting because elsewhere the absurdity of the rhymed couplets had ironic effect. Here the rhyme seems merely silly, as if to reflect the lack of thought Prufrock intends to put into the things he does as an old man.

There are stories of mermaids falling in love with human men. This reference also echoes the emotional frustration expressed by the earlier sea image of the "pair of ragged claws."

Line 135

Eliot uses this image of the mermaids to signal that Prufrock has come close to experiencing something wonderful and magical and strange, but that Prufrock ultimately fails to believe that the singing he has heard will ever be for him.

Lines 136-138

The image in these three lines of Prufrock remaining distant and apart from the emotional life he desires adds meaning to the preceding lines. Prufrock as an old man walking along the beach and remembering that he had actually at one time seen the mermaids, as well as heard their singing, is especially poignant, and helps us see him as someone in crisis.

The words "seen" and "seaward" echo the earlier "silent seas" of line 81.

Lines 139-141

The use of the first person plural might be convincing confirmation of the reading of "The Love Song of J. Alfred Prufrock" as a soliloquy or interior monologue of a divided self. Eliot uses the image of the sea and "sea-girls," and the repetition of "singing," as well as the associations now accumulated around the word "overwhelming" (with its meanings of "submerging" and "engulfing") to symbolize the deeply emotional place which Prufrock could not reconcile with human life in the real world, thus necessitating the division in himself.

It is another of Eliot's ironic touches that Prufrock's "lovesong" could only be sung to him by human voices that would wake his divided self to drown in the sea of his own emotions.

Themes

Alienation and Loneliness

In this poem, the speaker's poor ability to relate to other people, especially women, has him playing out a long dialogue in his mind, consisting of fragments of his past that are so intensely personal that he does not bother to connect them into a logical flow. The "us" he refers to in the first stanza is himself, which tells us that he is a person who is accustomed to being alone, to addressing another part of his mind in the way a more social person would talk to a friend. One of the strongest indications of his loneliness is the repeated use of questions to himself: he is so desperately alone in his thought that he examines every little aspect about his behavior, so curious about what people will think of him that he asks the only person he can talk to about it, the one person who knows no more than himself. This is a sign of social inexperience. In the eighth stanza, he imagines that the stares of others will pin him to the wall for inspection, the way an insect is held in place, "pinned and wiggling." He is so deeply immersed in his loneliness, so tragically alienated, that he fears even the first basic action that would bridge the gap between another person and himself: eye contact.

The main cause of his alienation is his low selfesteem, causing him to shrink in embarrassment from other people at the same time that he is wondering if he might not deserve better, if he is not setting his aims too low. Critics have pointed to the lines "I should have been a pair of ragged claws / Scuttling across the floors of the silent seas" as an indication of Prufrock's attitude toward women, exploring it in dozens of ways, from literary allusions to the sexual practices of crayfish in Eliot's native St. Louis. Regardless of the lines' origins, it is clearly an image that isolates the speaker, and the use the words "ragged" and "scuttling" define a fantasy in which the speaker clearly does not think well of himself.

Time

Balanced against Prufrock's morbid introversion—his fear that entering a relation with the woman he is on his way to meet will entangle him too deeply in the drab, mundane things of the world—is the fear that time is slipping away from him and making him old. He worries about losing his hair and losing the youthful muscle in his arms and legs, which drives him forward to do what he set out to do, and yet he hesitates because of the suspicion that the situation is not entirely drastic yet. After the third stanza establishes for us the fact that Prufrock is familiar with the dark, seamy side of life, the fourth stanza contains his constant self reassurances that "there will be time ...," indicating that he is worried that all of life's mysteries (the fog, murder, creation) will be over once he has made it to his destination. There will be "time yet for a hundred indecisions" he tells himself, afraid that he is going to lose the luxury of infinite possibility. He knows, though, that time will narrow his possibilities down one by one, systematically making each possibility real or not real: having already seen the eternal Footman, Death, he is familiar that there will not be time for everything. Although Prufrock is not sure that he wants to commit to comfort, a world of "sunsets and teacups and sprinkled streets," he knows that the time he has for indecision is not limitless, and he fears that waiting too long will leave him a lonely old man, sitting in the window, smoking.

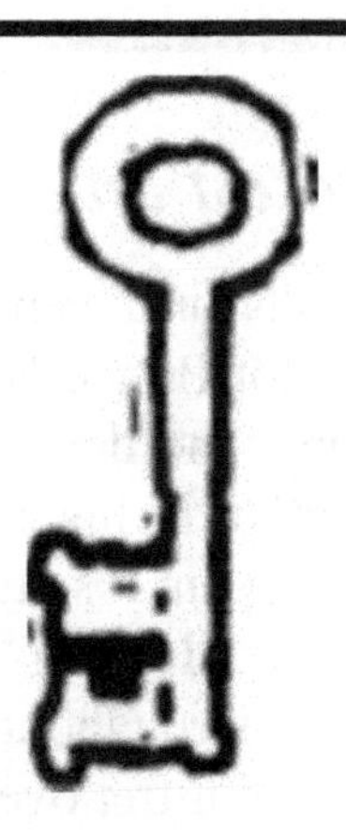

Topics for Further Study

- Rewrite this poem as a short story, covering one night in the life of Prufrock. Where does he go? What does he see that makes him bring up the subjects that he does? In your story, who will you have Prufrock talking to?

- Read Alfred, Lord Tennyson's poem "Ulysses," also included in *Poetry for Students*. What does Prufrock have in common with Ulysses? What similarity can you draw between the two poems' styles?
- Do you think Prufrock has a good sense of who he is, or do you think he is deluded? Give evidence to support your answer.

Doubt and Ambiguity

Near the end of the poem Prufrock declares, "I am not Prince Hamlet, nor was I meant to be." To many, the defining characteristic of Shakespeare's Hamlet is his inability to conquer or accept his doubts and settle upon one course of action to follow. Having seen Prufrock's thought process twist throughout stanza after stanza, and having seen him fret over whether the life he is committing to is the one he really wants, or if he has chosen unwisely because of social pressure, or if his body is so worn out that he has no choice left at all, the reader could rightly disagree with him and say "Yes," he is too Hamlet. The indecisiveness of Hamlet is clearly there: what he seems to be denying is the "Prince" part of the identity, as if the title of royalty is too glamorous for a humble fool like himself. Ironically, it is this self-consciousness, this constant reminder that he is a lowly being, that conflicts with his rebellious nature and causes Prufrock the most indecisiveness. Near the middle of the poem his constant questioning of himself takes on a brief pattern: "how should I presume?" he asks, and after another stanza he asks again, followed at the end of the following stanza with "should I presume?" In this sequence we see that his self-questioning, his long one-man dialogue that is meant to think things through and settle some issues, is actually working backward, taking him further from decision. In this poem the speaker's doubts do not reach an answer, they just multiply, so when he finally decides to take action it is not with comfort or certainty but with regret; he sees his move from contemplation to action as a drowning.

Style

"The Love Song of J. Alfred Prufrock" begins with an epigraph, a quote that sets the tone for the poem to follow. This epigraph, included in the poem in the original Italian, is from Dante's *Divine Comedy*. Its use here emphasizes Eliot's belief in the instructive function of poetry, as well as his conviction that it was a poet's responsibility to be aware of and build on the established tradition of poetry.

This poem (exclusive of the epigraph) is structured into four sections, with each section separated by an ellipsis, a mark used in conventional punctuation to indicate an omission, but used here to signal either time passing between thoughts relevant to the subject under consideration, or information considered too obvious to be included.

Eliot's belief that "No verse is free for the serious poet" is apparent in "The Love Song of J. Alfred Prufrock." This poem is written in free verse with varying line lengths, but Eliot employs rhyme as a major structural component in its composition.

In fact, in the 131 lines of the main poem structure, only 12 lines are unrhymed. Note the pattern of the rhyme in the first stanza, beginning "Let us go then, you and I....": a couplet—an unrhymed line—a series of three couplets—an unrhymed line—a couplet. Such a pattern serves to establish coherence in the stanza, as well as to create a distinctive music.

Eliot also found repetition useful to establish rhythms of ideas as well as sound rhythms. Note the repetition of the word "time" in the two stanzas beginning "And indeed there will be time...." in the first section.

Conventional punctuation and sentence structure are used in this poem, but capital letters at the beginnings of lines stress lineation, thus balancing the importance of the sentence with the importance of the line. While Eliot maintained that poetry should conform to current conversational speech, he emphasized the musical qualities of speech, as well as the imagistic and symbolic possibilities of words, by his use of lineation.

The varying line lengths and stanza lengths of this poem are indicative of Eliot's refusal to impose a form on the thoughts and emotions at the center of the composition. It was not his purpose to discover or create a new form for poetry, but to free the poet from set forms in order to allow each poem to create its own form—in this case a "love song" which Eliot sings onto the page for the reader.

Historical Context

In a review of *Catholic Anthology 1914-15,* edited by the poet Ezra Pound and containing "The Love Song of J. Alfred Prufrock," critic Arthur Waugh noted that if "the unmetrical, incoherent banalities of these literary 'Cubists' were to triumph, the State of Poetry would be threatened with anarchy." His remarks are clearly intended to frighten lovers of poetry and to dismiss the authors as bungling amateurs. Little could Waugh have guessed that he was identifying the very effects that the poets intended, and that his criticism is only of interest to us today because it signifies that, by the time he was writing, the Modern Age had arrived. Modernism is a blanket term that we use for a great number of artistic and philosophical movements (including Cubism in painting) that were intent on throwing away the old standards and replacing them with work that is closer to the way the people really live and think.

This struggle between life and theory has always gone on and continues to this day. In music, for example, rap has been embraced by its listeners as an authentic expression of how people feel, but it is scoffed at by music connoisseurs for its lack of melodic complexity—"incoherent banalities," as Waugh would say. After years of being underground and rejected, rap has now reached a level of acceptance that makes it a prime target to be dismantled by the next new upstarts. Similarly, the rise of Modernism was a reaction to Victorianism, which was a reaction to Romanticism, and on throughout history. Since the chain is unbroken, there is no clear place to start tracing Modernism's roots, but one good place might be in 1798, with the publication of William Wordsworth's and Samuel Taylor Coleridge's *Lyrical Ballads*. In response to the formal, strict poetry that had come before him, Wordsworth wrote that poetry should drawn from "a selection of language really used by man." Poetry, he felt, was too far out of touch with reality, and he encouraged writers to change the way they thought about their job. Out of this grew the Romantic movement, which included such great early-nineteenth century writers as Keats, Shelley, Byron, Tennyson, Emerson, Melville, Poe, and Dickinson. Romanticism was a spirit of intellectual freedom that affected all areas of society. The individual, especially the artistic individual, was held to be of the highest importance to Romanticism: creativity was worshipped.

The last half of the nineteenth century saw the triumph of industry and capitalism, and is considered a less humanistic time. Novels concerned themselves with social structure, and poetry became more formal, more stylized, emphasizing how things were said over what was said. The Industrial Revolution brought trains and eventually automobiles, stepping up the pace of life: reading became less and less relevant, a luxury to be enjoyed by those who were socially comfortable. Throughout the period, though, there were scattered elements that would eventually make it impossible for the forces of social order to hold: Marx and Engels published *The Communist Manifesto* in 1848; Darwin published *Origins of the Species* in 1859; Freud's *The Interpretation of Dreams* came out in 1900. Each of these created a revolution in its own intellectual area and lead to the Modernist suspicion of all previously accepted beliefs.

There is no particular philosophy of Modernism, but instead we measure its growth by looking at various revolutionary movements in the arts. In 1909, for instance, the Futurist movement in Italy released its "Foundation Manifesto of Futurism" (bold artistic movements often announce themselves with manifestoes), praising "aggressive action, the mutual leap, the punch and slap." At the same time, Pound fell in with a group of poets in London and discussed principles that eventually became known as Imagism, known for its rejection of poetic conventions. Pound was also instrumental in founding Vorticism, which was based on change and motion and was supposed, Pound said, to "sweep out the past century as surely as Attila swept across Europe." These three examples of literary movements at the time give us a sense of the new values that came with Modernism: embracing instead of avoiding the industrial world; an emphasis on powerful, not pretty, poetry; a willingness to use any tools and break any rules in order to capture what the world was really like; in general, a devotion to a higher social cause (think of all of those manifestoes) and an unwillingness to simply create art for its own sake.

Compare & Contrast

- **1915:** The first long-distance telephone call from New York to San Francisco was made. Alexander Graham Bell repeated the words he spoke in 1868 over the first working model ("Mr. Watson, come here ...") to Thomas Watson in San Francisco. The call took 23 minutes to go through.
  Today: International telephone calls, as well as cellular communications and public phones on airplanes, all are transmitted by having their signals bounced off of satellites orbiting the earth.
- **1916:** The new Ku Klux Klan was organized, taking its name from a 1860s group and receiving an official charter from the state of Georgia. Throughout the following fifty years, the Klan was responsible for a reign of terror against non-whites and non-Catholics, committing lynchings and firebombings across the south with little interference from the law.
- **1957:** The first Civil Rights Act to be passed by Congress since the 1870s made it a federal crime to

discriminate against people because of race.

Today: The Ku Klux Klan is still in operation, despite strong public opposition.

Critical Overview

According to Vincent Miller, "By 1914 the age of the heroic achiever was over. That was ... the truth [this] love song pinned down in a startlingly new and creative way for an entire generation." Indeed, American poet John Berryman declares that "Modernist poetry begins" in the simile "like a patient etherised upon a table." He recognizes, however, that even the title manifests a decidedly Modernist "split" in its juxtaposition of the full romance of the term "love song" against such a highly formalized name as J. Alfred Prufrock. This is a technique Eliot discovered in reading the French Symbolist poets Jules Laforgue and Charles Baudelaire. He declared that his early free verse was "more 'verse' than 'free,'" adopting Laforgue's practice of "regularly rhyming lines of irregular length, with the rhyme coming in irregular places." This creates the music of "The Love Song of J. Alfred Prufrock," and inspired American poet Delmore Schwartz to theorize that "[t]here is [a mode of] poetry whose chief aim is that of incantation, of inducing a certain state of emotion." It is clearly the intent of "The Love Song of J. Alfred Prufrock" to involve the reader at an emotional level, and Eliot's use of the second person "you" in the opening line is an expert strategy toward this. But whether the "you" Prufrock is speaking to begins as the poet Eliot or as some imaginary companion, it is evident that, as

Northrop Frye maintains, Prufrock ultimately is talking to himself, and that "[i]n addressing a 'you' who is also himself the pattern is set for a division between Prufrock and the world he contemplates—until he stands irrevocably separated from that world.

M. L. Rosenthal contends that "The Love Song of J. Alfred Prufrock Prufrock" projects "an actual inner state ... of one type of cultivated American psyche of Eliot's generation." He further notes "a strongly adolescent flavor," asserting that the poem "positively sweats panic at the challenge of adult sexuality and of living up to one's ideal of what it is to be manly in any sort of heroic model." Ann P. Brady says that Eliot was aware of this, maintaining that the poem reflects Prufrock back "from the world in which he moves" in a "clinically hard" way, and that this contrast with romantic aspirations—the "juxtaposition of lyricism with the tone of satire"—creates the Modernist tension. She finds the satire unusually effective in Eliot's coupling of rhyme words that "are absurd," particularly "ices crisis, platter-matter, flicker-snicker," producing what she calls "deflation by association."

English novelist May Sinclair notes Eliot's concern with reality, with his careful presentation "of the street and the drawing-room as they are," as well as "[w]ith ideas ... that are realities and not abstractions...." Thus "Prufrock" presents not only a man in the world but, as James F. Knapp says, "a mind shaped along the lines of [Modernist] depth psychology...." He sees this reflected in the poem by the abandonment of "logical continuity" necessitated by Eliot's material. The radicalness of "Prufrock," according to Knapp, is not simply in its break with poetic tradition, but in its use of old conventions and new ones to keep poetry "in touch with a changing world."

Sources

Ackroyd, Peter, *T.S. Eliot: A Life,* Simon & Schuster, 1984.

Berryman, John, "Prufrock's Dilemma," in *The Freedom of the Poet,* Farrar, Straus, 1976, pp. 270-78.

Brady, Ann P., *Lyricism in the Poetry of T. S. Eliot,* Kennikat, 1978.

Frye, Northrop, *T. S. Eliot,* Oliver and Boyd, 1963.

Grant, Michael, ed., *T.S. Eliot: The Critical Heritage,* Routledge, 1982.

Kenner, Hugh, *The Invisible Poet: T.S. Eliot,* McDowell, Oblinsky, 1959.

Knapp, James F., "Eliot's 'Prufrock' and the Form of Modern Poetry," in *Arizona Quarterly,* Vol. 30, No. 1, Spring, 1974, pp. 5-14.

Miller, Vincent, "Eliot's Submission to Time," in *Sewanee Review,* Summer, 1976, pp. 448-64.

Rosenthal, M. L., "Adolescents Singing, Each to Each—When We and Eliot Were Young," in *The New York Times Book Review,* October 20, 1985, pp. 3, 37.

Sinclair, May, '"Prufrock and Other Observations': A Criticism," in *The Little Review,* Volume IV, December, 1917, pp. 8-14.

Schwartz, Delmore, "The Literary Dictatorship of

T. S. Eliot," in *Partisan Review*. Vol. XVI, No. 2, February, 1949, pp. 119-37.

For Further Study

Blythe, Hal, and Charlie Sweet. "Eliot's 'The Love Song of J. Alfred Prufrock.'" *The Explicator* Volume 52, number 3, Spring 1994, p. 170.

> It would have seemed that by the time this was written all that needed to be said about the poem would have been covered, but these authors bring to light new information about different interpretations and possible sources for the "ragged claws" line.

Bradbury, Malcom. *The Modem World: Ten Great Writers*. New York: Viking Penguin Inc., 1988.

> Eliot is one of the great writers given his own chapter in this book, of course, but just as interesting is the introduction, which puts these ten writers (including Ibsen, Proust, Pirendello and Kafka) into perspective of one another like pieces of a jigsaw puzzle.

Symons, Julian. Makers of the New: The Revolution in Literature 1912-1939. New York: Random House, 1987.

> The author is a well-known biographer and critic who knew several of the important artistic figures discussed in this book, and

who therefore sketches out the rise of Modernism as an interesting, personal story.

CPSIA information can be obtained
at www.ICGtesting.com
Printed in the USA
BVHW062311310322
632891BV00009B/1801